NATURAL WORLD

LION

HABITATS • LIFE CYCLES • FOOD CHAINS • THREATS

Bill Jordan

WAYLAND

WWF

Produced in Association with WWF-UK

NATURAL WORLD

• Elephant • Giant Panda • Great White Shark
ller Whale • Lion • Polar Bear • Tiger

Produced for Wayland Publishers Limited by
Roger Coote Publishing
Gissing's Farm, Fressingfield
Suffolk IP21 5SH, UK

First published in 1999 by
Wayland Publishers Limited
61 Western Road, Hove
East Sussex BN3 1JD, England

All Wayland books encourage children to read and help them improve their literacy.

✓ The contents page, page numbers, headings and index help locate specific pieces of information.

✓ The glossary reinforces alphabetic knowledge and extends vocabulary.

✓ The further information section suggests other books dealing with the same subject.

Find Wayland on the Internet at http://www.wayland.co.uk

Cover: An adult male lion.
Title page: A lioness and her cub.
Contents page: A young lioness.
Index page: Cubs drinking at a waterhole.

WWF is a registered charity no. 201707
WWF-UK, Panda House, Weyside Park
Godalming, Surrey GU7 1XR

British Library Cataloguing in Publication Data
Jordan, Bill
  Lion: habitats, life cycles, food chains, threats. -
  (Natural world)
  1.Lions - Juvenile literature
  I.Title
  599.7'57

ISBN 0 7502 2445 2

Picture acknowledgements
Bruce Coleman Collection 6 (Gerald Cubitt), 9 (Gunter Ziesler), 11 (Jen & Des Bartlett), 14 (Mr Johnny Johnson), 15 (Christer Fredriksson), 18 (Janos Jurka), 24 (Norman Owen Tomalin), 26 (Erwin & Peggy Bauer), 27 (Gunter Ziesler), 30 (Peter Davey), 31 (Erwin & Peggy Bauer), 33 (HPH Photography), 34–5 (Uwe Walz), 35 (Leonard Lee Rue III), 37 (Werner Layer), 44m (Gunter Ziesler), 45t (Erwin & Peggy Bauer); Digital Vision 3, 6–7, 8, 12, 17, 19, 20, 23, 28–9, 32, 36, 44t, 45b; CM Dixon 41; Mary Evans Picture Library 40–41; Still Pictures 1 (Fritz Polking), 10 (M&C Denis-Huot), 13 (Yann Arthus-Bertrand), 16 (Nicholas Granier), 20–21 (M&C Denis-Huot), 22 (Nicholas Granier), 28 (Fritz Polking), 38 (M&C Denis-Huot), 39 (M&C Denis-Huot), 42 (Michel Gunther), 43 (Dylan Garcia), 44b (Yann Arthus-Bertrand), 45m (M&C Denis-Huot), 48 (Andrew Lewis); Tony Stone Images *front cover*. Artwork by Michael Posen.

Printed and bound by G. Canale & C.S.p.A., Turin, Italy

Contents

Meet the Lion

The lion is often called the King of Beasts. People have admired and feared this powerful creature for thousands of years. But because of their fear, humans have also hunted and killed lions.

▼ An adult male lion.

LION FACTS

The lion's scientific name is *Panthera leo*.

•

Lions live in groups called prides.

•

Lions are related to tigers, leopards, and other big cats, and to domestic cats.

•

When lions roar, the noise they make is so loud it can be heard 8 kilometres away.

Tail
A lion's tail measures 60–100 centimetres long.

Eyes
Good eyesight, especially
for spotting movement.

Mane
Only male lions
have manes.

Nose
Lions have an excellent
sense of smell.

Teeth
A lion has 30 teeth, shaped
perfectly for killing prey and
tearing flesh from the bone.

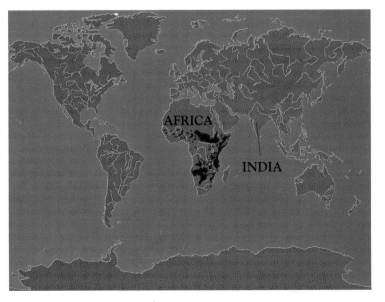

▼ The red shading on this map shows where
lions live in the wild.

AFRICA

INDIA

Legs
Powerful legs and
claws can catch,
hold and pull down a
buffalo more than
twice the lion's size.

Where do Lions Live?

Lions are members of the cat family. All these cats have evolved from the first type of cat, called *Pseudaelurus* (pronounced 'su-day-lure-us'), which lived around 20 million years ago.

Fifteen thousand years ago, lions were widespread in Africa, India, the Far East and even in parts of Europe. In Asia, lions are now found only in a nature reserve in the Gir Forest of north-west India.

▲ An Asian lion in the Gir Forest, India.

In Africa, lions live in the grasslands and woodlands of East, West and southern Africa, south of the Sahara desert. Some also live in deserts, such as the Kalahari desert in southern Africa. There are no lions left in the wild anywhere else. This book will follow the life cycle of an African lion.

▼ Four African lion cubs wait for their mother to return from hunting.

A Lion is Born

It is nearly time for the lioness to give birth. The cubs have been growing inside her for just over three months. This is quite a short time for such a large animal: cows and humans are pregnant for nine months.

◀ A lioness with her newborn cub.

LION CUBS

A newborn lion cub weighs about 1–1.5 kilograms.

●

There are usually two or three cubs in a litter, but there can be as few as one or as many as six.

Finally, after sixteen weeks of pregnancy, the lioness gives birth to her young. Their eyes are closed tight. Their light-brown coats have brownish-black spots over their bodies and legs, almost like a leopard. They will lose these markings once they reach about ten months old.

The lioness has found a secret den in which to give birth, which is well hidden and easily protected. She had a good idea of where to look for shelter after seeing older members of her pride do the same.

▲ These young cubs are hiding in the den where they were born.

A Lion's First Weeks

When they are six to nine days old, the cubs open their eyes. Their first teeth come through when they are three weeks old. All this time they are hidden in the secret den and the mother stands guard, except when she is hunting with the other females of the pride.

More than half of the cubs will not live to become adults. Some are killed by predators such as hyenas when the lioness is away. Others are killed by adult male lions that have recently joined the pride. Some cubs may die of starvation if there is not enough prey.

▲ Newborn cubs drink milk from their mother's four teats as often as they can.

▶ If the lioness senses danger, she may move her cubs from the den to a safer place. She carries them in her mouth, holding them by the scruff of the neck.

Joining the Pride

Eventually, when they are about eight weeks old, the lioness will bring the cubs out from the hidden den to join the pride. If they are lucky and there are plenty of kills, the cubs will begin to eat solid food. The mother keeps a watchful eye on her cubs. They are safe with other females around. The other females will allow the cubs to suckle them if they have milk, even if the cubs are not their own.

▼ Two lionesses with their cubs. Lions may rest for up to twenty hours a day.

▲ This fully grown male lion doesn't seem to enjoy the cub's game.

Females in a pride tend to give birth at the same time, so lion cubs are reared with other cubs of similar ages. The cubs soon begin to play. The females don't mind this, but males are likely to growl at the cubs to warn them off.

The lioness calls her cubs with a soft growl and they respond with high whimpering sounds. If the pride moves, the cubs can follow because the adults move at a slow pace. The young ones get their first canine teeth, the big ones at each side used for tearing meat, when they are fifteen weeks old.

Growing Up

Female lions that are related to each other live together in prides. This means that the young cubs are related to most of the other lions in the pride.

▲ A group of lionesses resting in the branches of a tree.

The growing cubs are now relatively safe from predators. But they are often jostled out of the way when they try to eat. The cubs have to snatch a bite when they can and enjoy what is left, as long as the adults haven't eaten it all.

A lot of time is spent resting and dozing in the shade during the day to keep cool and to save energy. At night the pride goes off hunting and the cubs have to remain quiet and hidden until they return.

▼ The adults have not left much of this animal carcass for these cubs to eat.

Protecting the Territory

Each pride has a territory that varies in size from 15 to 160 square kilometres, depending on the number of prey animals. The males patrol the territory and mark it by spraying their urine on bushes and rocks. This is called scent marking.

ADULT MALE LIONS

A fully grown male measures about 3 metres from nose to tail and weighs about 250 kilograms.

●

Adult male lions are about 50 per cent bigger than adult females.

▼ Male lions show their power by roaring, mainly at night and early in the morning.

▲ Male lions in the pride protect the pride's territory from other males.

The pride usually consists of between four and twelve related females of varying ages, along with their young ones, and between one and four unrelated males.

Male lions are powerful animals. They have a large mane which makes them look bigger and more threatening. The mane also protects the lion's neck from claws and teeth during fights.

17

Young lions have to struggle to survive as they grow up. It is not until they are eighteen months old that they begin to share a kill with the adults. If there are not many kills, they starve.

▲ Young lions join in the feast after a buffalo is killed.

Driven Away

The females stay with the pride, but the males are driven out and forced to fend for themselves when they are two or three years old. The male lions still cannot hunt at this age, so if they stayed on, they would deprive the younger cubs within the pride of food. They will leave as a group and become wanderers, trying to keep clear of the large males in other territories.

▼ These two young male lions have been driven away from their pride.

Learning to Hunt

Cubs sometimes practise attacking the kill when the adults are not too hungry. But the process of learning to hunt doesn't begin until they are old enough to join the pride in a hunt. Even then, at first they stay back and watch the adults.

▼ A group of lionesses wait for night-time before going hunting.

In the pride, hunting is done by the lionesses and not the lions. They hunt by sight rather than by smell. If there is enough moonlight, lionesses usually hunt at night when it is cooler.

▼ Lions can hunt at night because they have very good eyesight.

Lions can run at up to 58 kilometres per hour, but only for short distances. Many of the animals they hunt can run much faster. So lions have to get quite close to their prey to have any chance of success.

How Lions Hunt

When choosing their prey, lionesses usually pick a medium-sized animal such as a wildebeest, weighing 150–200 kilograms. The lionesses slowly creep towards the wildebeest. As they move forward, they keep their bodies close to the ground, using long grass and bushes for cover.

When she is close enough, one lioness will make a dash for the prey. The animal will see her at once. Alarmed, it will turn and run for its life, across the path of another lioness who will then attack. The prey will see the danger and swerve again. If it is lucky it will escape.

▲ A lioness creeping slowly towards her prey. She keeps low to stay out of sight.

22

If the animal is unlucky it will turn and run into more danger. Another lioness will dash towards it, give it a powerful blow and knock it to the ground. Then, avoiding its thrashing legs, she will grab its throat and wrestle it to the ground. The lioness may kill her prey by biting its neck or throat. Or she might suffocate it by forcing its mouth and nose shut with her jaws.

▼ This lioness is running at full speed to stop a warthog escaping.

What do Lions Eat?

As well as wildebeest, lions like to eat zebras, antelopes and gazelles. Occasionally a lion will tackle a large and powerful buffalo if there is no other prey available. They often single out sick, young or injured animals which are easier to kill.

▼ When attacking a zebra, lions have to be careful because a well-placed kick from a fully grown zebra could smash a lion's skull or break its jaw or ribs.

HUNTING FACTS

Lions are mainly nocturnal, which means they do their hunting at night and rest during the day.

•

Lions often eat only every other day.

•

Lionesses kill 20–30 big animals each year.

LION FOOD CHAIN

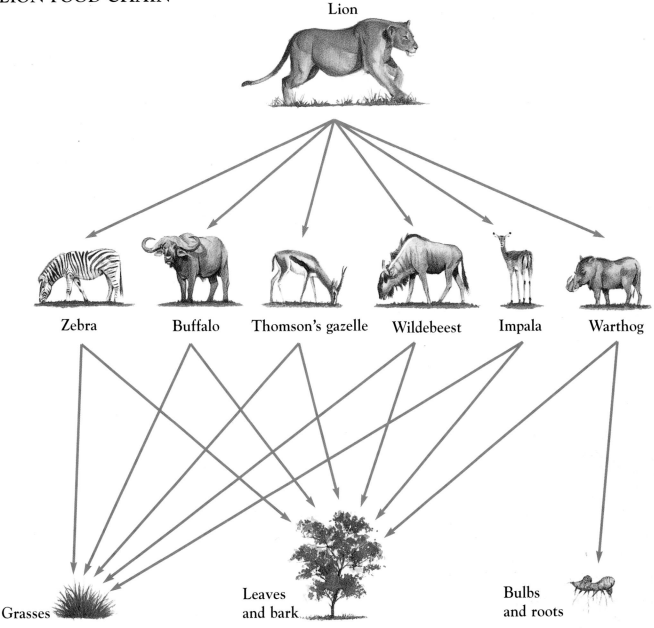

Lion

Zebra   Buffalo   Thomson's gazelle   Wildebeest   Impala   Warthog

Grasses

Leaves and bark

Bulbs and roots

Lions will also kill and eat smaller animals such as lizards, rats and birds. They often kill these creatures by breaking the neck with a swipe from a paw. If hunting is not successful, lions may steal prey from leopards and even hyenas.

▲ The lion is at the top of its food chain. Adult lions don't have any natural predators.

Feeding

Although the male may not take part in the hunt, he will feed before the females and cubs. A male needs 7 kilograms of meat per day, but he can eat as much as 80 kilograms if he is very hungry.

▲ A male lion eating a zebra that has been killed by the lionesses in the pride.

The lionesses all feed together when the male has finished eating. There is very little squabbling among them. Lions have a very rough tongue. This acts like a comb to hold the flesh while they bite off pieces.

▼ A lioness cleans her cub after feeding.

▲ These two lionesses have caught a large buffalo.

Food Shortages

When grasses and other plant foods run short, animals such as wildebeest, which lions feed on, migrate in search of better food. The lions are left with only warthog, topi and buffalo on which to survive.

The vast herds of migrating wildebeest, zebra and antelope, numbering many thousands of animals, may have to cross a large river. They look for places where the banks are not too steep and the river is not too deep. Lions know this is their opportunity for easy hunting and they lie in wait. Eventually, after many successful attacks, they become so full of meat they lose interest.

▼ To reach fresh food supplies, wildebeest often have to cross rivers.

Leaving Home

Survival is very hard for the young males when they first leave home. They are not experienced hunters so they are hungry most of the time. If it is one young male on his own he may not survive unless he can join forces with one or more lions in the same situation. Together as a group they have a much better chance of making a kill or stealing a kill from a leopard or hyenas.

▼ Two young male lions. They will probably have to hunt together to catch enough food to survive.

▲ These two young males killed an impala in a muddy waterhole. Now they are cleaning each other.

The young males will stay together as a group for one or two years. All this time they are growing up. Their chests get deeper and their muscles larger as they become fully grown lions. Very often the male cubs that were born together will remain as a group throughout their lives.

32

◀ When a lion tries to kill a porcupine, the spines can stick in the lion's skin. If the wounds get infected, the lion may die.

▼ This male lion can smell another male nearby.

At first, the young males have to hunt small, slow animals. They soon discover how difficult it is to get through the shell of a tortoise or the spines of a porcupine.

Groups of young males try to avoid getting into fights with other prides when they wander into their territories. Slowly they grow bigger and stronger and gain more courage. Once they are old enough, they will start to seek out other lions' territories to take over.

33

Fighting for Territory

Lions become mature at about three or four years of age. They begin to look for a pride that they can take over by driving away the resident males. If there is just one dominant male in the pride that they attack, they will stand a chance. There is often serious fighting when they attack.

Lions defend their territory with all their strength. Even if one lion is left alone and finds his group's territory threatened, he will fight to protect the land. Sometimes females will join in to support their male, but if they see that the male will not win, they may retreat.

▼ A lioness warns off a male that has come into her pride's territory.

If the resident male is killed, or badly injured and driven away, the newcomers take over the pride. If there are several adult males in the pride, the newcomers may be taught a hard lesson and driven off or badly injured. Large wounds usually become infected and cause death.

▲ This male lion was injured in a fight with another male.

Head of the Pride

The resident male or males will not usually give up without a fight and if the newcomers threaten the cubs, the females will defend them furiously. Large groups of males usually beat smaller groups in battles for a pride. There may be as many as nine lions in a large group.

▲ A large male roars to tell other males that he is the head of his pride.

▶ These two males are looking for a pride to take over.

KILLING THE YOUNG

It is not unusual for the incoming male who takes over a pride to kill all the young cubs. He does this to get rid of all traces of the previous male. Then all the new cubs that are born in the pride will be related to him.

Within the pride all the females are related. The male is only related to his offspring: If he is a single male in the pride, without the support of other lions, he will soon be driven out. In fact, he may be the head of his pride for no more than two years. As he grows old and loses his strength, he will be driven out by incoming stronger males. When this happens, he won't survive for long afterwards. But if there are several males they can usually keep a pride for up to ten years.

Mating

Lions will fight together as a group to gain control of a pride. But when they want to mate with a lioness, they will compete against each other, although it is rare for them to fight.

When a lion finds a lioness to mate with he will stay close by her for four or five days, warning off male competition, until he mates with her. Mating takes place more than once a year and any time during the year. It is not seasonal like most prey animals in Africa.

▶ A male and a female preparing to mate.

▼ This male is roaring to attract a female, while a cub looks on.

Threats

During the last 100 years, many lions have been hunted and killed by people. Most of the hunters were settlers from Europe, who killed lions and other wild animals for sport.

▼ A European hunter (on the far right) takes aim at a lion. This drawing was made about 100 years ago.

LIONS IN ANCIENT ROME

Lions were still in North Africa less than 2,000 years ago. The Romans caught them to use in gladiator shows, and to kill Christians. In the rest of Africa and parts of India, lions were safe at that time.

▼ This wall carving shows Roman gladiators fighting against a lion, a lionesss and a bear. Thousands of lions were killed in shows like this in ancient Rome.

41

▲ The city in the distance of this photo is Nairobi, the capital of Kenya. As Africa's population grows, lions and other animals are being pushed into smaller areas, closer to where people live.

◄ Many animals that lions hunt are killed and used as food for humans, called 'bush meat'. This sometimes means that there is not enough food left for the lions.

Today, lions are being pushed out of their habitats all the time. As the number of people in the world increases, more land is farmed and built upon. Each lion pride needs a large territory, but there is less and less space for them.

In many countries, lions are regarded as pests. When they come into conflict with people, lions are often shot, trapped or poisoned.

Lions are now on the endangered species list. If you want to help protect them, you could join a conservation group. There is a list of addresses on page 47.

Lion Life Cycle

 Usually between one and six cubs are born three months after the lion mates with the lioness. The cubs are born with brownish-black spots and light-brown coats. The cubs suckle from their mother soon after they are born.

 The cubs open their eyes at around six to nine days old and they get their first teeth at three weeks old. During this period they are hidden in the den where they were born.

 At eight weeks old, the cubs join the pride and can eat solid foods. The mother keeps a watchful eye on the cubs who are beginning to learn to play.

4. At around two or three years old, the males are forced out of the pride to fend for themselves. They often form groups and hunt together. Females stay within the pride for their entire lives.

5. At three or four years old, male lions become sexually mature. They compete to be head of the pride. Once they are part of a pride they mate with females.

6. Lions can live to around twenty-five years old.

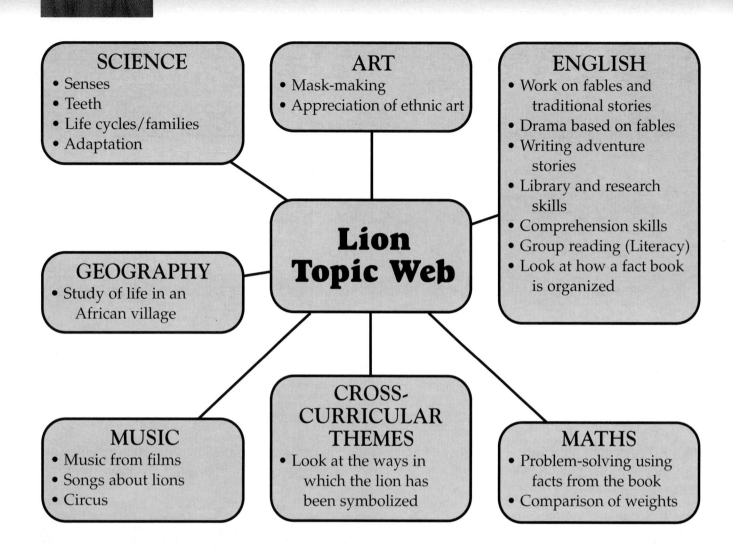

SCIENCE
- Senses
- Teeth
- Life cycles/families
- Adaptation

ART
- Mask-making
- Appreciation of ethnic art

ENGLISH
- Work on fables and traditional stories
- Drama based on fables
- Writing adventure stories
- Library and research skills
- Comprehension skills
- Group reading (Literacy)
- Look at how a fact book is organized

GEOGRAPHY
- Study of life in an African village

Lion Topic Web

MUSIC
- Music from films
- Songs about lions
- Circus

CROSS-CURRICULAR THEMES
- Look at the ways in which the lion has been symbolized

MATHS
- Problem-solving using facts from the book
- Comparison of weights

Extension Activities

English
- Adjectives: make alphabet books of adjectives about lions.
- Write a lion diary using facts from the book.
- A book study, e.g. *The Butterfly Lion* by Michael Morpurgo.

Art
- Using photographs of a lion's habitat, discuss and extend previous work on colour mixing.

Science
- Focus for P.S.E work about 'Growing up'.
- Focus for extended work about classification – carnivores, omnivores and herbivores.

IT
- Use graphics software to design posters to support work on conservation, or a film or book study.

Glossary

Canine teeth Long, pointed teeth at the front of a lion's jaws. There are two in the top jaw and two in the bottom jaw.

Carnivore A meat-eating animal.

Den A secret place.

Distemper A very infectious disease usually affecting dogs.

Dominant The strongest animal in a group.

Gladiator A person in ancient Rome who fought wild animals or other gladiators to entertain people.

Habitat The natural home for an animal or plant.

Mane Long hair on the neck of some animals.

Mature Grown up.

Migrate Move from one area to another at certain times of the year.

Offspring Another word for children or young.

Predator An animal that hunts another animal for food.

Prey An animal hunted by another animal for food.

Pride A group of lions.

Resident A word describing the male lion or lions that control a pride and defend it against other males.

Scent A smell left by an animal.

Starvation When something dies because it does not have enough food.

Suckle When a female animal produces milk for her young. The young drink from their mother's teats.

Territory An area inhabited and defended by an animal or group of animals.

Further Information

Organizations to Contact

Care for the Wild International
1 Ashfolds, Horsham Road,
Rusper, West Sussex RH12 4QX
Tel: 01293 871596
Web site:
www.careforthewild.org.uk

WWF-UK
Panda House, Weyside Park
Godalming, Surrey GU7 1XR
Tel: 01483 426444
Web site: www.wwf-uk.org

Web Sites

The Asiatic Lion Information Centre
www.wkweb4.cableinet.co.uk/alic/
This site has information and news about Asian lions, and lots of links to other lion web sites.

The Lion Research Center
www.lionresearch.org/
News, maps and information on the scientific and conservation projects being carried out by the Lion Research Center.

Books to Read

Animal Atlas (Dorling Kindersley, 1992)

Animals of the Grasslands by Stephen Savage (Wayland, 1996)

Lions by Claire Robinson (Heinemann, 1998)

Lion and Tiger by Rod Theodorou (Heinemann, 1996)

Nature at Risk by Sally Morgan (Kingfisher, 1995)

1001 Facts About Wild Animals by Moira Butterfield (Kingfisher, 1992)

Index

All the numbers in **bold** refer to photographs or illustrations.